# This belongs to:

**Her Name:** _____

**His Name:** _____

©BRILLIANCEANDRESILIENCE

# Forever One

**THE DAY WE GOT MARRIED** _____

## MY FAVORITE PARTS ABOUT THAT DAY

| *His* | *Hers* |
|---|---|
|  |  |

# Forever One

WHERE WE HONEYMOONED _____

## MY FAVORITE PARTS ABOUT THAT TRIP

### His

### Hers

# Forever One

## WHAT DID YOU THINK ABOUT MARRIAGE, THAT TURNED OUT TOTALLY DIFFERENT?

*His*

*Hers*

# Forever One

## WHAT IS SOMETHING YOU LEARNED ABOUT YOUR SPOUSE DURING MARRIAGE?

*His*

*Hers*

# Forever One

## WHAT IS A NEW WAY YOU HAVE FOUND TO SHOW YOUR LOVE TO EACH OTHER?

*His*

*Hers*

# Forever One

## WHAT IS SOMETHING THAT YOUR SPOUSE IS REALLY WONDERFUL AT?

*His*

*Hers*

# Forever One

## WHAT IS YOUR FAVORITE MEMORY OF THE LAST YEAR TOGETHER?

**His**

**Hers**

# Forever One

## WHAT WAS YOUR FAVORITE DATE TOGETHER FROM THIS PAST YEAR?

### His

### Hers

# Forever One

## WHAT CELEBRATION STOOD OUT TO YOU THE MOST?

*His*

*Hers*

# Forever One

## WHAT WAS BAD AT THE TIME, BUT YOU LAUGH ABOUT NOW?

### His

### Hers

# Forever One

## WHAT IS THE GREATEST ACHIEVEMENT YOU EXPERIENCED?

### His

### Hers

# Forever One

## IF YOU COULD RELIVE ONE DAY OF THE LAST YEAR, WHICH ONE WOULD IT BE?

### His

### Hers

# Forever One

## WHAT MADE THIS PAST YEAR CHALLENGING?

*His*

*Hers*

# Forever One

## WHEN WE WERE A GREAT TEAM, WHAT WERE WE DOING?

| His | Hers |
|-----|------|
|     |      |

# Forever One

## WHAT IS OUR GREATEST STRENGTH AS A COUPLE?

### His

### Hers

# Forever One

## HOW DID WE HANDLE CONFLICT THIS LAST YEAR?

| His | Hers |
|-----|------|
|     |      |

# Forever One

## WHAT DID WE START DOING LAST YEAR THAT YOU'D LIKE US TO CONTINUE?

### His

### Hers

# Forever One

## WHAT IS SOMETHING YOU WOULD LIKE TO IMPLEMENT INTO OUR MARRIAGE?

*His*

*Hers*

# Forever One

## WHEN WERE YOU MOST PROUD OF YOUR SPOUSE THIS PAST YEAR?

### His

### Hers

# Forever One

## WHEN DO YOU THINK YOUR SPOUSE IS AT THEIR BEST?

| His | Hers |
|---|---|
|   |   |

# Forever One

## HOW HAVE YOU FELT LOVED BY YOUR SPOUSE THIS PAST YEAR?

### His

### Hers

# Forever One

## HOW HAVE YOU HANDLED THE UNKNOWNS IN MARRIAGE?

### His

### Hers

# Forever One

## WHAT IS SOMETHING YOU WANT TO COMMIT TO WITH YOUR SPOUSE IN THE NEXT YEAR?

### His

### Hers

# Forever One

## WHAT ARE THREE THINGS YOU HAVE ON YOUR BUCKET LIST AS A MARRIED COUPLE?

*His*

*Hers*

# Forever One

## HOW CAN YOU MAKE YOUR SPOUSE'S DAY BETTER?

### His

### Hers

# Forever One

## WHERE IS GOD IN YOUR MARRIAGE?

| *His* | *Hers* |
|---|---|
|  |  |

# Forever One

## WHAT SAINTS DO YOU ASK FOR INTERCESSION IN YOUR MARRIAGE?

| His | Hers |
|---|---|
|   |   |

# Forever One

## HOW ARE WE GOING TO FOCUS OUR FAITH TOGETHER GOING FORWARD?

### His

### Hers

# Forever One

## WHERE DID YOU NOT FEEL GOD IN YOUR MARRIAGE?

### His

### Hers

# Forever One

## WHAT DO YOU PRAY FOR WITHIN YOUR MARRIAGE?

### His

### Hers

# Forever One

## GOD GAVE US THE GIFT OF INTIMACY IN MANY WAYS. WHAT ARE SOME WAYS YOU FEEL CLOSE TO ONE ANOTHER?

| His | Hers |
|---|---|
|  |  |

# Forever One

## WHAT DO THE GOOD DAYS LOOK LIKE?

| His | Hers |
|---|---|
| | |

# Forever One

## WHAT DO THE BAD DAYS LOOK LIKE?

### His

### Hers

# Forever One

## WHAT ARE YOUR FAVORITE SCRIPTURE READINGS? WHY?

### His

### Hers

# Forever One

## HOW WERE YOU BRAVE THIS YEAR?

### His

### Hers

# Forever One

## WHO DO YOU RELY ON IN LIFE OTHER THAN YOUR SPOUSE?

| His | Hers |
|---|---|
|  |  |

# Forever One

## WHO DO YOU SEEK COUNSEL FROM? LIST AS MANY AS YOU CAN.

### His

### Hers

# Forever One

## WHAT MARRIED COUPLE INSPIRES YOU TO BE HOLIER?

### His

### Hers

# Forever One

## WHAT LAY PEOPLE INSPIRE YOU TO BE HOLIER?

| His | Hers |
|-----|------|
|     |      |

# Forever One

**DO YOU HAVE A SPIRITUAL MENTOR, COUNSELOR OR PRIEST TO WALK WITH YOU PERSONALLY?**

*His*

*Hers*

# Forever One

## WHAT PARTS OF YOUR MARRIAGE DO YOU STRUGGLE WITH THE MOST?

### His

### Hers

# Forever One

## HOW OFTEN DO YOU PRAY FOR THAT SPECIFIC THING?

| His | Hers |
|---|---|
|   |   |

# Forever One

## WHO ARE PEOPLE OUTSIDE OF YOUR MARRIAGE WHO LOVE YOU?

**His**

**Hers**

# Forever One

## WHEN WAS A TIME YOU FELT LESS THAN, AND YOUR SPOUSE HELD YOU UP?

### His

### Hers

# Forever One

## WHEN WAS A TIME THAT YOU HAD TO BE FORGIVEN BY YOUR SPOUSE?

| His | Hers |
|---|---|
|   |   |

# Forever One

## WHAT IS SOMETHING YOU WANT YOUR SPOUSE TO KNOW AND YOU HAVEN'T TALKED ABOUT IT YET?

### His

### Hers

# Forever One

## HOW DO YOU FEEL ABOUT THE POSSIBILITY OF CHILDREN IN THE NEAR FUTURE?

**His**

**Hers**

# Forever One

## WHAT ARE YOU MOST SCARED OF WITH A FUTURE FAMILY?

### His

### Hers

# Forever One

## WHAT ARE YOU MOST SCARED OF FOR THE FUTURE?

**His**

**Hers**

# Forever One

## WHO DO YOU TRUST THAT WILL WALK WITH YOU THROUGH A FAMILY LIFE?

*His*

*Hers*

# Forever One

## WHAT IS THE BEST PART OF THE INTIMACY THAT GOD GAVE US?

### His

### Hers

# Forever One

## WHAT IS THE HARDEST PART OF THE MARITAL ACT?

### His

### Hers

# Forever One

## HOW HAS YOUR PERSONAL LIFE CHANGED SINCE GETTING MARRIED?

*His*

*Hers*

# Forever One

## WHAT IS YOUR FAVORITE THING TO DO WITH YOUR SPOUSE?

### His

### Hers

# Forever One

## HOW HAS YOUR WORKING LIFE BEEN SINCE YOU'VE GOTTEN MARRIED?

| His | Hers |
|---|---|
|   |   |

# Forever One

## WHAT STRUGGLES DO YOU SEE WITH BOTH HAVING JOBS?

### His

### Hers

# Forever One

## HAVE YOU WELCOMED ANY PETS INTO YOUR HOME? IF SO, WHAT IS THE BEST PART?

*His*

*Hers*

# Forever One

## WHAT IS THE HARDEST PART?

### His

### Hers

# Forever One

## HOW DO YOU FEEL GOD IS CALLING YOU TO A MORE INTIMATE RELATIONSHIP WITH HIM?

### His

### Hers

# Forever One

## WHERE DO YOU FEEL THAT GOD IS CALLING YOU TO GIVE YOUR SURRENDER?

### His

### Hers

# Forever One

## HOW DO YOU KNOW GOD LOVES YOU? GIVE SOME EXAMPLES

| His | Hers |
| --- | --- |
|  |  |

# Forever One

## WHERE DO YOU THINK GOD IS DESIRING TO HEAL YOU IN YOUR LIFE AND MARRIAGE?

**His**

**Hers**

# Forever One

## REFLECT IN PRAYER ON THE BEATITUDES TO APPLY TO YOUR MARRIAGE.

### His

What do you think Jesus is saying to you?

How do you think he wants to bring you closer to Him?

What does He want you to know?

### Hers

What do you think Jesus is saying to you?

How do you think he wants to bring you closer to Him?

What does He want you to know?

# Forever One

**"BLESSED ARE THE POOR IN SPIRIT, FOR THEIRS IS THE KINGDOM OF HEAVEN"**

## His

## Hers

# Forever One

"BLESSED ARE THE MEEK, FOR THEY SHALL POSSESS THE LAND"

## His

## Hers

# Forever One

## "BLESSED ARE THOSE WHO MOURN, FOR THEY SHALL BE COMFORTED"

*His*

*Hers*

# Forever One

"BLESSED ARE THEY WHO HUNGER AND THIRST FOR JUSTICE, FOR THEY SHALL HAVE THEIR FILL"

## His

## Hers

# Forever One

"BLESSED ARE THE MERCIFUL, FOR THEY SHALL OBTAIN MERCY"

## His

## Hers

# Forever One

## "BLESSED ARE THE CLEAN OF HEART, FOR THEY SHALL SEE GOD"

*His*

*Hers*

# Forever One

**"BLESSED ARE THE PEACEMAKERS, FOR THEY SHALL BE CALLED CHILDREN OF GOD"**

*His*

*Hers*

# Forever One

"BLESSED ARE THEY WHO SUFFER PERSECUTION FOR JUSTICE' SAKE, FOR THEIRS IN THE KINGDOM OF HEAVEN.

## His

## Hers

# Forever One

## HOW ARE YOU CALLED BE A HUMBLE SERVANT TO THE LORD?

*His*

*Hers*

# Forever One

AFTER A YEAR OF MARRIAGE, RESTATE YOUR VOWS, AND NEW ONES AS A COMMITMENT TO YOUR SACRIFICIAL LOVE FOR EACH OTHER.

## His

# Forever One

## After a year of marriage, restate your vows, and new ones as a commitment to your sacrificial love for each other.

### Hers

## Credits

Written by: Abigail Gartland with inspiration of the Holy Spirit
Clipart: Lana Elanor & DigitalParadiseUSA

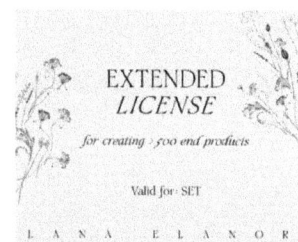

# About the Author

## Abigail Gartland

I love my faith. The idea for sharing this reflection on the first year of a catholic marriage came from lots of friends and family in my life entering the sacrament of marriage. As I watch my friends and family learn the beauties, graces, struggles, and. hardships of marriage, I have prepared through prayer a reflection on the first year of marriage. Each book is dedicated to very special couples in my life who have enriched my faith in different ways. I am blessed to have written this reflection with the unending support of my friends and family. When I am not writing, I am a middle school teacher, as well as an author for The Little Saint Books series. I hope you enjoy this reflection. I pray for each and every couple who opens this book to lean into Jesus for the support of you marriage.

*Abbie*

www.ingramcontent.com/pod-product-compliance
Lightning Source LLC
LaVergne TN
LVHW070539070526
838199LV00076B/6811